ROALD DAHL

CREATIVE WRITING

with

FANTASTIC MR FOX

How to Write a **Marvellous** PLOT

PUFFIN

PUFFIN BOOKS is part of the Penguin Random House group of companies
whose addresses can be found at global.penguinrandomhouse.com.

Published by Penguin Random House Children's UK: 80 Strand, London WC2R 0RL

Penguin Random House Australia Pty Ltd: 707 Collins Street, Melbourne, VIC 3008

Penguin Random House New Zealand: 67 Apollo Drive, Rosedale, Auckland 0632

First published 2020

001

Written by James Clements

Copyright © The Roald Dahl Story Company Ltd / Quentin Blake, 2020.

ROALD DAHL is a registered trademark of The Roald Dahl Story Company Ltd.

www.roalddahl.com

With thanks to Michelle Porte-Davies

Moral rights asserted

Printed in China

ISBN: 978–0–241–38461–9

Contents

This **Roald Dahl** symbol is used to highlight examples and ideas from his stories – in this case, *Fantastic Mr Fox*. If you read and understand these examples, they will help you to become an even better writer!

What if?

The events that happen in a story are called the **plot**. As the author, you are in charge of the plot of your story. Anything can happen to your characters – exciting things, funny things or downright strange things. It's up to you!

Use your imagination to complete these *What if . . . ?* questions. Do they help you to think of a plot for your story? Use the ideas box for extra help.

What if the Earth was visited by

_____ from space?

What if people could change into

_____ ?

What if, instead of going to school, children

went to _____ ?

What if _____

could talk?

What if you found some magical

_____ ?

Every evening as soon as it got dark, Mr Fox would say to Mrs Fox, "Well, my darling, what shall it be this time? A plump chicken from Boggis? A duck or a goose from Bunce? Or a nice turkey from Bean?"

What if . . . a fox decided to take some food from three nasty farmers?

What if . . . the farmers wanted to stop him?

IDEAS BOX

aliens	books	toys
wizards	space	vegetables
pets	work	the jungle
crystals	robots	the sea

You can start creating your plot by thinking about the characters. **Draw a character below. Label anything that's special about them. What could happen to them in your story?**

What if my character _____

_____?

Thinking about the setting can help you to decide what happens in your story. Your plot can take place somewhere you know, or it could happen somewhere that's from your imagination. **Write two setting ideas below.**

A place you know well:

_____

What could happen there?

_____

_____

A place you've invented:

_____

What could happen there?

_____

_____

RD

On a hill above the valley there was a wood.

In the wood there was a huge tree. Under the tree there was a hole.

In the hole lived Mr Fox and Mrs Fox and their four Small Foxes.

Where is it? A hole under a tree in a wood.

What could happen there? Some foxes could be trapped by some nasty farmers!

5

Plot types

There are lots of different **types of story**, from funny stories and adventure stories, to mystery stories and sad stories.

Different types of stories have different sorts of plots, but most stories have:

★ a **beginning**, to introduce the characters and set the scene.

★ a **middle**, where different things happen to the characters.

★ an **end**, where we find out how things turn out for the characters.

Use the Story Machine below to think of some new plots. You can add your own characters and plot ideas to the machine as well.

Fantastic Mr Fox
A tiny dinosaur
A kind pirate
A superhero
A magical creature
An ordinary child
A giant
An animal
_____
_____

wants to find food for
wants to hide
wants to escape from
wants to defeat
wants to be
wants to be friends with
wants to hide from
_____
_____
_____
_____

his little children.
an enchanted crystal.
their twin sister.
a new planet.
her home.
a talking animal.
Farmer Boggis.
a robot from space.
a new child at school.
_____
_____

Use the Story Machine to choose a character and plot idea.
Plan your idea below.

In many stories, there is one big problem that the hero has to overcome.
What big problem could your hero have? How will they solve it?

RD

The noise he heard now was the most frightening noise a fox can ever hear – the scrape-scrape-scraping of shovels digging into the soil.

Character: Fantastic Mr Fox

Wants: To find food for his little fox children

Big problem: The farmers are waiting to catch him.

Solution: He digs tunnels so the farmers don't see him.

Character: _____

Wants: _____
_____
_____
_____

Big problem: _____
_____
_____
_____

Solution: _____
_____
_____
_____

Brilliant beginnings

All good stories need an **opening** – something to capture the reader's attention and set the scene. The opening introduces the characters and setting.

Read the description below from the opening of *Fantastic Mr Fox*. **Circle the words that help you to imagine the farmers.**

They were rich men. They were also nasty men. All three of them were about as nasty and mean as any men you could meet. Their names were Farmer Boggis, Farmer Bunce and Farmer Bean.

Choose one of your Story Machine characters from page 6, or think of a new character. Write a story opening that describes them to the reader. Use the ideas box for extra help.

_____

_____

_____

_____

_____

_____

IDEAS BOX

- **What is your character's name?**
- **What does your character look like?**
- **What should the reader know about them?**
- **What are they doing at the start of the story?**

It can be exciting to start your story with some action. **Use your imagination to continue the story openings below.**

Crash! The door opened and _____

_____ .

The footsteps grew louder. The boy turned round and saw _____

_____ .

Lightning flashed across the sky and _____

_____ .

When a character speaks out loud, it is called **dialogue**. This is another good way to open your story. **Choose one of your Story Machine ideas from page 6. Write a line of dialogue to open the story in the speech bubble below.**

Exclamations are sentences that end with an exclamation mark. Could you start your story with an exclamation?

"Dang and blast that lousy beast!"

"Dig for your lives!"

"Go on, beat it!"

"This is my private pitch!"

RD

TOP TIP

If your story starts with some action, your reader doesn't need to understand exactly what is happening. A mysterious opening will make them want to read on!

Clever connectives

A **connective** is a word that links two words or phrases together.

Changing the connective can change the meaning of a sentence.

> The farmers were angry **because** Mr Fox stole from them.
>
> The farmers were angry **so** Mr Fox stole from them.

Sometimes a connective stops a sentence making sense.

> The farmers were angry **which** Mr Fox stole from them.

IDEAS BOX

and	which
but	since
so	until
because	while
if	although
unless	or
that	however

Choose a connective and complete the sentence for each picture.
Use the ideas box for extra help.

Mr Fox was clever _____

_____ .

Mr Fox began to dig quickly _____

_____ .

Then, Mr Fox stood up _____

_____ .

Pick two different connectives to complete the sentences below, so each one means something different. Can you draw an illustration for each sentence?
Use the ideas box on page 10 for extra help.

Mr Fox couldn't sleep _____
Rat was running around.

Mr Fox couldn't sleep _____
Rat was running around.

You can also use connectives to help you think of new plot ideas.
Finish the sentences below, as if each one was the start of a story.

There was a puff of smoke and _____.

There was a puff of smoke but _____.

There was a puff of smoke because _____.

There was a puff of smoke so _____.

Read your sentences again. Which would make the best start to a story?
Write what happens next.

_____

_____

_____

_____

_____

Magnificent middles

The middle of a story is often where the plot develops and exciting or funny things happen. There are new **problems** for the hero to solve, and there are usually plenty of surprises, too.

Here are four middle-of-the-story problems. **Finish them with your own ideas.**

_____ gets stuck in _____.

_____ has an argument with _____.

_____ cannot find _____.

_____ is chased by _____

The same situation can be funny or exciting, depending on your story. In both examples below, a character falls off his chair. **Draw a circle around the funny story and a zigzag shape around the adventure story.**

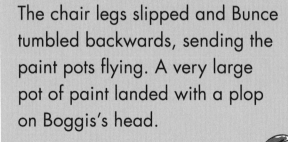

The blast threw Bunce backwards, smashing his chair into pieces on the concrete floor. Unsteadily he rose to his feet.

The chair legs slipped and Bunce tumbled backwards, sending the paint pots flying. A very large pot of paint landed with a plop on Boggis's head.

Choose your favourite middle-of-the-story problem from page 12.

Plan what happens in the scene. Will you make it exciting, funny, or both?

Now, write the scene you have chosen.

_____

_____

_____

_____

_____

_____

_____

_____

Action scenes

There is often plenty of action in the middle of the story. Action scenes are written with lots of different **verbs**, or doing words.

Carefully chosen verbs can make an action scene more exciting.
What exciting verbs could you use in a chase scene?

hurrying

verbs

*"Quick!" said Mr Fox. "**Hide!**" He and Badger and the Smallest Fox **jumped** up on to a shelf and **crouched** behind a row of big cider jars.*

R**D**

Imagine the hero of your story is being chased. **Write a description of what happens, and use some of the exciting verbs you thought of above.**

_____

_____

_____

_____

_____

You can create excitement by repeating words or phrases, too. Read the extract below. Now, imagine your hero is sneaking past a sleeping guard. **Use repeated words or phrases to capture the excitement. Use the ideas box for extra help.**

_____

_____

_____

_____

_____

_____

_____

_____

RD

"Go downwards!" ordered Mr Fox. "We've got to go **deep**! As **deep** as we possibly can!"

The tunnel began to grow **longer** and **longer**. It sloped steeply downward. **Deeper** and **deeper** below the surface of the ground it went.

IDEAS BOX

- slowly, slowly
- centimetre by centimetre
- carefully, ever so carefully
- softly, softly
- nearer and nearer
- closer and closer

Worst-possible moment

Many stories build up to a **climax**.
Often, this is a moment where it looks
like all is lost. Writing a worst-possible
moment into your story can make
it really exciting!

Read the extract from *Fantastic Mr Fox*. It looks like Mr Fox is going
to be caught stealing, just when Mr Fox's family need him to bring
them some food and drink!

*Peering around the jars, they saw a huge woman coming down into
the cellar. At the foot of the steps, the woman paused, looking to right
and left. Then she turned and headed straight for the place where
Mr Fox and Badger and the Smallest Fox were hiding. She stopped
right in front of them. The only thing between her and them was a
row of cider jars. She was so close, Mr Fox could hear the sound of
her breathing. Peeping through the crack between two bottles, he
noticed that she carried a big rolling-pin in one hand . . .*

*The woman in the cellar reached out and lifted a jar of cider from
the shelf. The jar she took was next but one to the jar behind which
Mr Fox was crouching.*

*"I'll be glad when the rotten brute is killed and strung up on the
front porch," she called out.*

How do you feel as you read this part of the story?

_____

_____

_____

_____

Look at the extract again. **Underline any words and
phrases that show you Mr Fox is in trouble.**

How could Mr Fox escape? **Write what might happen next.**

_____

_____

_____

_____

_____

Lots of different things could be the worst-possible moment for the hero of your story. **Write some ideas in the space below.**

worst-possible moment

Choose your favourite idea for your hero's worst-possible moment. **Write a paragraph to describe the moment.**

_____

_____

_____

_____

_____

Excellent endings

Every story needs a good ending!
In most stories there is a **resolution**,
where the reader finds out what
happens to the characters.

**Draw a line to match the different characters from _Fantastic Mr Fox_ to
the right endings.** If you haven't read the story yet, which ending do
you think they should have?

Mr Fox and the other
animals . . .

. . . are left waiting by
the foxhole, with the rain
trickling down their necks.

Farmers Boggis,
Bunce and Bean . . .

. . . live safely in an
underground village, and
every day they eat like kings.

The farmers, Boggis, Bunce and Bean, are nasty and mean.
What else could happen to give them the ending they deserve?

_____

_____

_____

_____

_____

_____

_____

Think of a fair ending for each of these characters.

a footballer who stopped to help
a player on the opposite team

an evil wizard who has been using
his magic to steal treasure

a brave police officer who chased
and caught a scary burglar

a girl who took her younger brother's
ice cream

Not all stories end with a resolution. Some stories
end on a **cliffhanger**, where the reader doesn't
know what is going to happen next. **Write a
cliffhanger ending for one of the characters above.**

TOP TIP
Making up a great
ending can be tricky.
Try to surprise your
reader with something
unexpected!

Perspective and tense

Stories are told in different ways. Some are told from the **perspective**, or point of view, of the **first person**. This is where a character talks directly to the reader. Others are told from the perspective of the **third person**. This is where a narrator describes what is happening to the characters.

Mr Fox crept up the dark tunnel to the mouth of his hole. He poked his long handsome face out into the night air and sniffed once.

He moved an inch or two forward and stopped. He sniffed again. He was always especially careful when coming out from his hole.

RD

Roald Dahl tells the story of *Fantastic Mr Fox* in the third person. **Read the extract above. Now, continue the scene in the first person, as if you were Mr Fox.**

I crept up the dark tunnel to the mouth of the hole. I _____

_____

_____

_____

_____

_____

_____

_____

Stories are told in different tenses, too. The **past tense** tells us what has already happened, while the **present tense** tells us the story as it is happening.

Mr Fox **examined** the wall carefully. He **saw** that the cement between the bricks **was** old and crumbly, so he **loosened** a brick without much trouble and **pulled** it away.

Complete the chart below to show the verbs in the present tense and the past tense.

Present tense		Past tense
Mr Fox **examines**	→	Mr Fox examined
Mr Fox **sees**	→	_____
_____	←	the cement **was**
_____	←	he **loosened**
he **pulls**	→	_____

In the story extract above, Mr Fox pulls a brick out of a wall. What might he see through the hole? **Describe the scene using the present tense.**

He sees _____

_____

_____

first person
third person
past tense
present tense

Choose one perspective and one tense from the box. Imagine Mr Fox is going for a walk in a place you know really well. **Write about his walk, using the perspective and tense you have chosen.**

_____

_____

_____

_____

_____

Other perspectives

Stories don't always need to be told
from the narrator or hero's perspective.
Sometimes it is interesting to see things
from a **different character's perspective**.

In *Fantastic Mr Fox*, Roald Dahl sometimes shows us what the foxes are doing, and sometimes he shows us what the farmers are doing. Sometimes, we even see the same scene from two different points of view!

Read the extract below. **Use one colour to underline the part that is from Mr Fox's perspective. Use another colour to underline the part that is from Boggis, Bunce and Bean's perspective.**

It was a small silver speck of moonlight shining on a polished surface. Mr Fox lay still, watching it. What on earth was it? Now it was moving. It was coming up and up . . . Great heavens! It was the barrel of a gun! Quick as a whip, Mr Fox jumped back into his hole and at that same instant the entire wood seemed to explode around him. Bang-bang! Bang-bang! Bang-bang!

The smoke from the three guns floated upward in the night air. Boggis and Bunce and Bean came out from behind their trees and walked towards the hole.

"Did we get him?" said Bean.

RD

In this extract, Mr Fox and the Small Foxes arrive in Boggis's Chicken House Number One. How do you think the chickens would feel about the foxes arriving in their house? **Note your ideas below.**

The Small Foxes went wild with excitement. They started running around in all directions, chasing the stupid chickens.

RD

Write the scene from the perspective of one of the chickens.

_____

_____

_____

_____

_____

_____

_____

_____

_____

_____

_____

_____

TOP TIP

Try writing a scene in your story from an unexpected perspective – perhaps from a minor character, a pet or even a piece of furniture!

Planning a story

There are lots of ways to **plan a story**, but thinking carefully about the plot first is always useful.

Write the plot of *Fantastic Mr Fox* in the boxes.
If you haven't read the story, decide how you would write it! Use the ideas box for extra help.

1
Opening

2
Action

3
Worst-possible moment

4
Resolution

IDEAS BOX

- The farmers want to stop Mr Fox stealing from them.
- Mr Fox is almost captured.
- The animals dig secret tunnels to get food from the farms.
- The animals have a big feast.
- Mr Fox steals food from the farmers to feed his family.

5
Ending

Now, try writing the plot for another story you know well. It could be from a fairy tale, your favourite film or even another Roald Dahl book.

1 Opening

2 Action

3 Worst-possible moment

4 Resolution

5 Ending

TOP TIP

Don't forget – you're the author. If you want to change the story, then you can!

Mighty maps

Maps can be a great way of planning your story. They help you to think about where each **scene** will take place.

In *Fantastic Mr Fox*, the animals build "a little underground village, with streets and houses on each side – separate houses for Badgers and Moles and Rabbits and Weasels and Foxes". **Can you draw a map of the village in the space below?**

Look at your map. Can you think of any new stories that could take place there? **Write some *What if . . . ?* questions below.**

What if Mr Fox _____?

What if a baby rabbit _____?

What if all the moles _____?

Draw a new map as the setting for your own story.
Use the ideas box for extra help.

IDEAS BOX

- an overgrown forest
- inside a computer game
- an undersea world
- a strange planet
- a secret school

What stories could happen in the world you have created? **Note your ideas below.**

Storyboards

Another fantastic way of mapping out a story is through drawing a comic strip or **storyboard**. This can help you to plan each scene in your story.

TOP TIP

You don't have to fill in your storyboard in order. You might find it easier to plan the beginning and ending first, and then work out the middle.

Choose one of your story ideas from page 27.
Use the storyboard below to draw or write a plan for your story.

Choose your favourite scene from the storyboard. Now, write out the scene below.

Tremendous titles

You can choose a **title** at any stage. It could be after you've planned the plot, or even when the story is finished! Sometimes thinking of a title first can help you to plan the story.

Think of some great story titles and write them in the space below. Use the ideas box for extra help.

Ali and the Cheesecake Moon

Look at the titles you thought of above. **Which title is:**

. . . **the funniest?** _____

. . . **the scariest?** _____

. . . **the most exciting?** _____

You are a writer!

Use the boxes below to start planning a new story. You could look back over the ideas you've had in this book, think of a new idea or use the Story Machine on page 6.

1
Opening

2
Action

3
Worst-possible moment

4
Resolution

5
Ending

Top tips

- You are in charge of your plot. If you can imagine it, you can include it!

- When planning your plot, it can be helpful to draw pictures, maps or a storyboard. Try asking *What if…?* questions or thinking about the ending.

- A strong opening to your story is very important – this is where you introduce your characters and setting, and capture your reader's attention.

- Think about what will happen to your main character. What kind of problems might they have to solve? Would you like them to be happy or sad in the end?

- Make sure you include some action in your story. It might be funny, exciting or sad, but every good story needs some drama.

- You can end your story however you like, but the story does need a clear ending – even if it is a cliffhanger.

- Stories can be told in the past tense or the present tense.

- You might choose one character to tell your story, or you could tell different parts of the story through the eyes of different characters.

- A funny or clever title will make people want to pick up your story and read it.

- Planning your story first is very useful, but remember that you don't have to stick to your plan. You can change the story and add new parts in as you go!

My marvellous plot

Use the balloons to plan a marvellous plot for your story.

There is a set of balloons in every **Roald Dahl Creative Writing** book.

Join each set together to write a terrific story of your own!

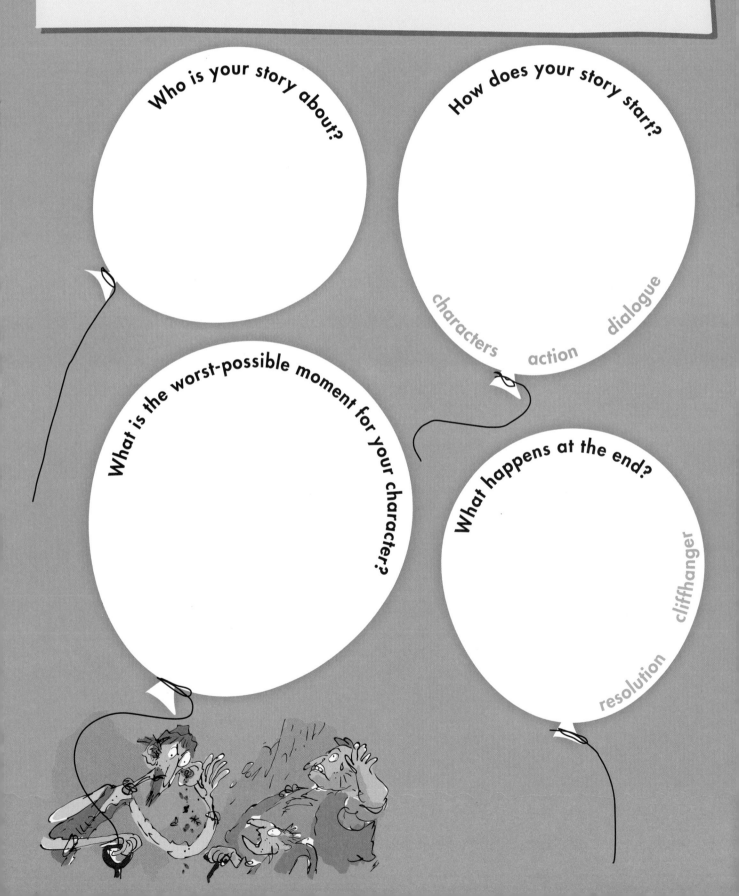

Who is your story about?

How does your story start?

characters   action   dialogue

What is the worst-possible moment for your character?

What happens at the end?

cliffhanger

resolution